Camping Color By Numbers Coloring Book
Large Print Wildlife, Cute Kids, Beautiful Wilderness, Adorable Animals, And Scenic Forests, Lakes and Mountains

By Color Questopia

Thank you
for your purchase!

**Claim your FREE digital copy of our
Highlight Reel Color By Number Book:**

Check out our website: colorquestopia.com

**Join our Facebook group:
facebook.com/colorquestopia**

Follow us on Instagram: @colorquestopia

**Did you enjoy this book?
Please leave us a review!**

https://geni.us/cqreview

Color By Number Tips

1. Relax and have fun

Let your cares slip away as you color the images. Take your time. Coloring is a meditative activity and there's no wrong way to do it. Feel free to color as you listen to music, watch TV, lounge in bed- do whatever relaxes you most! You can also color while you're out and about- on the train or at a cafe- take the book with you anywhere you go. Coloring is therapeutic and is great for stress relief and relaxation!

2. Colors corresponding to each number are shown on the back cover of the book - THIS BOOK HAS OUR NEW COLORING SYSTEM WHERE EVERY COLOR IN EVERY BOOK IS SHOWN ON THE BACK OF THE BOOK

Each number corresponds to a color shown on the back of the book. Because this is our new system, there may be colors and numbers on the back that aren't in this book- that's totally okay. Just follow the numbers on the images in this book, and match those numbers to colors. You can match the color as closely as you like- but feel free to change the color or the shade if you don't have the exact color match- that's totally fine. Although this is a color by number book, it's completely okay to get creative and color the images with whichever colors you like and have. The numbers are there to be a guide and to allow you to color without having to focus your energy on choosing colors.

3. Choose your coloring tools

Everyone has their favorite coloring markers, crayons, pencils, pens- even paints! Feel free to color with any tool that you like! If you choose markers or paints, we recommend putting a blank sheet of paper or cardboard behind each image, so that your colors don't run onto the next image.

1. Black
2. Golden
3. Light Red
4. Medium Red
5. Red
6. Dark Red
7. Lemon Yellow
8. Light Yellow
9. Yellow
10. Dark Yellow
11. Bright Orange
12. Light Orange
13. Medium Orange
14. Orange
15. Dark Orange
16. Chocolate
17. Light Brown
18. Medium Brown
19. Brown
20. Dark Brown
21. Neon Green
22. Light Green
23. Medium Green
24. Green
25. Army Green
26. Dark Green
27. Peach
28. Light Pink
29. Medium Pink
30. Pink
31. Hot Pink
32. Dark Pink
33. Medium Purple
34. Purple
35. Light Violet
36. Soft Violet
37. Violet
38. Dark Violet
39. Baby Blue
40. Sky Blue
41. Light Blue
42. Medium Blue
43. Blue
44. Dark Blue
45. Navy Blue
46. Beige
47. Light Gray
48. Medium Gray
49. Gray
50. Dark Gray

1. Black
2. Golden
3. Light Red
4. Medium Red
5. Red
6. Dark Red
7. Lemon Yellow
8. Light Yellow
9. Yellow
10. Dark Yellow
11. Bright Orange
12. Light Orange
13. Medium Orange
14. Orange
15. Dark Orange
16. Chocolate
17. Light Brown
18. Medium Brown
19. Brown
20. Dark Brown
21. Neon Green
22. Light Green
23. Medium Green
24. Green
25. Army Green
26. Dark Green
27. Peach
28. Light Pink
29. Medium Pink
30. Pink
31. Hot Pink
32. Dark Pink
33. Medium Purple
34. Purple
35. Light Violet
36. Soft Violet
37. Violet
38. Dark Violet
39. Baby Blue
40. Sky Blue
41. Light Blue
42. Medium Blue
43. Blue
44. Dark Blue
45. Navy Blue
46. Beige
47. Light Gray
48. Medium Gray
49. Gray
50. Dark Gray

1. Black
2. Golden
3. Light Red
4. Medium Red
5. Red
6. Dark Red
7. Lemon Yellow
8. Light Yellow
9. Yellow
10. Dark Yellow
11. Bright Orange
12. Light Orange
13. Medium Orange
14. Orange
15. Dark Orange
16. Chocolate
17. Light Brown
18. Medium Brown
19. Brown
20. Dark Brown
21. Neon Green
22. Light Green
23. Medium Green
24. Green
25. Army Green
26. Dark Green
27. Peach
28. Light Pink
29. Medium Pink
30. Pink
31. Hot Pink
32. Dark Pink
33. Medium Purple
34. Purple
35. Light Violet
36. Soft Violet
37. Violet
38. Dark Violet
39. Baby Blue
40. Sky Blue
41. Light Blue
42. Medium Blue
43. Blue
44. Dark Blue
45. Navy Blue
46. Beige
47. Light Gray
48. Medium Gray
49. Gray
50. Dark Gray

1. Black
2. Golden
3. Light Red
4. Medium Red
5. Red
6. Dark Red
7. Lemon Yellow
8. Light Yellow
9. Yellow
10. Dark Yellow
11. Bright Orange
12. Light Orange
13. Medium Orange
14. Orange
15. Dark Orange
16. Chocolate
17. Light Brown
18. Medium Brown
19. Brown
20. Dark Brown
21. Neon Green
22. Light Green
23. Medium Green
24. Green
25. Army Green
26. Dark Green
27. Peach
28. Light Pink
29. Medium Pink
30. Pink
31. Hot Pink
32. Dark Pink
33. Medium Purple
34. Purple
35. Light Violet
36. Soft Violet
37. Violet
38. Dark Violet
39. Baby Blue
40. Sky Blue
41. Light Blue
42. Medium Blue
43. Blue
44. Dark Blue
45. Navy Blue
46. Beige
47. Light Gray
48. Medium Gray
49. Gray
50. Dark Gray

1. Black
2. Golden
3. Light Red
4. Medium Red
5. Red
6. Dark Red
7. Lemon Yellow
8. Light Yellow
9. Yellow
10. Dark Yellow
11. Bright Orange
12. Light Orange
13. Medium Orange
14. Orange
15. Dark Orange
16. Chocolate
17. Light Brown
18. Medium Brown
19. Brown
20. Dark Brown
21. Neon Green
22. Light Green
23. Medium Green
24. Green
25. Army Green
26. Dark Green
27. Peach
28. Light Pink
29. Medium Pink
30. Pink
31. Hot Pink
32. Dark Pink
33. Medium Purple
34. Purple
35. Light Violet
36. Soft Violet
37. Violet
38. Dark Violet
39. Baby Blue
40. Sky Blue
41. Light Blue
42. Medium Blue
43. Blue
44. Dark Blue
45. Navy Blue
46. Beige
47. Light Gray
48. Medium Gray
49. Gray
50. Dark Gray

1. Black
2. Golden
3. Light Red
4. Medium Red
5. Red
6. Dark Red
7. Lemon Yellow
8. Light Yellow
9. Yellow
10. Dark Yellow
11. Bright Orange
12. Light Orange
13. Medium Orange
14. Orange
15. Dark Orange
16. Chocolate
17. Light Brown
18. Medium Brown
19. Brown
20. Dark Brown
21. Neon Green
22. Light Green
23. Medium Green
24. Green
25. Army Green
26. Dark Green
27. Peach
28. Light Pink
29. Medium Pink
30. Pink
31. Hot Pink
32. Dark Pink
33. Medium Purple
34. Purple
35. Light Violet
36. Soft Violet
37. Violet
38. Dark Violet
39. Baby Blue
40. Sky Blue
41. Light Blue
42. Medium Blue
43. Blue
44. Dark Blue
45. Navy Blue
46. Beige
47. Light Gray
48. Medium Gray
49. Gray
50. Dark Gray

1. Black	26. Dark Green
2. Golden	27. Peach
3. Light Red	28. Light Pink
4. Medium Red	29. Medium Pink
5. Red	30. Pink
6. Dark Red	31. Hot Pink
7. Lemon Yellow	32. Dark Pink
8. Light Yellow	33. Medium Purple
9. Yellow	34. Purple
10. Dark Yellow	35. Light Violet
11. Bright Orange	36. Soft Violet
12. Light Orange	37. Violet
13. Medium Orange	38. Dark Violet
14. Orange	39. Baby Blue
15. Dark Orange	40. Sky Blue
16. Chocolate	41. Light Blue
17. Light Brown	42. Medium Blue
18. Medium Brown	43. Blue
19. Brown	44. Dark Blue
20. Dark Brown	45. Navy Blue
21. Neon Green	46. Beige
22. Light Green	47. Light Gray
23. Medium Green	48. Medium Gray
24. Green	49. Gray
25. Army Green	50. Dark Gray

1. Black
2. Golden
3. Light Red
4. Medium Red
5. Red
6. Dark Red
7. Lemon Yellow
8. Light Yellow
9. Yellow
10. Dark Yellow
11. Bright Orange
12. Light Orange
13. Medium Orange
14. Orange
15. Dark Orange
16. Chocolate
17. Light Brown
18. Medium Brown
19. Brown
20. Dark Brown
21. Neon Green
22. Light Green
23. Medium Green
24. Green
25. Army Green
26. Dark Green
27. Peach
28. Light Pink
29. Medium Pink
30. Pink
31. Hot Pink
32. Dark Pink
33. Medium Purple
34. Purple
35. Light Violet
36. Soft Violet
37. Violet
38. Dark Violet
39. Baby Blue
40. Sky Blue
41. Light Blue
42. Medium Blue
43. Blue
44. Dark Blue
45. Navy Blue
46. Beige
47. Light Gray
48. Medium Gray
49. Gray
50. Dark Gray

1. Black
2. Golden
3. Light Red
4. Medium Red
5. Red
6. Dark Red
7. Lemon Yellow
8. Light Yellow
9. Yellow
10. Dark Yellow
11. Bright Orange
12. Light Orange
13. Medium Orange
14. Orange
15. Dark Orange
16. Chocolate
17. Light Brown
18. Medium Brown
19. Brown
20. Dark Brown
21. Neon Green
22. Light Green
23. Medium Green
24. Green
25. Army Green
26. Dark Green
27. Peach
28. Light Pink
29. Medium Pink
30. Pink
31. Hot Pink
32. Dark Pink
33. Medium Purple
34. Purple
35. Light Violet
36. Soft Violet
37. Violet
38. Dark Violet
39. Baby Blue
40. Sky Blue
41. Light Blue
42. Medium Blue
43. Blue
44. Dark Blue
45. Navy Blue
46. Beige
47. Light Gray
48. Medium Gray
49. Gray
50. Dark Gray

1. Black
2. Golden
3. Light Red
4. Medium Red
5. Red
6. Dark Red
7. Lemon Yellow
8. Light Yellow
9. Yellow
10. Dark Yellow
11. Bright Orange
12. Light Orange
13. Medium Orange
14. Orange
15. Dark Orange
16. Chocolate
17. Light Brown
18. Medium Brown
19. Brown
20. Dark Brown
21. Neon Green
22. Light Green
23. Medium Green
24. Green
25. Army Green
26. Dark Green
27. Peach
28. Light Pink
29. Medium Pink
30. Pink
31. Hot Pink
32. Dark Pink
33. Medium Purple
34. Purple
35. Light Violet
36. Soft Violet
37. Violet
38. Dark Violet
39. Baby Blue
40. Sky Blue
41. Light Blue
42. Medium Blue
43. Blue
44. Dark Blue
45. Navy Blue
46. Beige
47. Light Gray
48. Medium Gray
49. Gray
50. Dark Gray

1. Black
2. Golden
3. Light Red
4. Medium Red
5. Red
6. Dark Red
7. Lemon Yellow
8. Light Yellow
9. Yellow
10. Dark Yellow
11. Bright Orange
12. Light Orange
13. Medium Orange
14. Orange
15. Dark Orange
16. Chocolate
17. Light Brown
18. Medium Brown
19. Brown
20. Dark Brown
21. Neon Green
22. Light Green
23. Medium Green
24. Green
25. Army Green
26. Dark Green
27. Peach
28. Light Pink
29. Medium Pink
30. Pink
31. Hot Pink
32. Dark Pink
33. Medium Purple
34. Purple
35. Light Violet
36. Soft Violet
37. Violet
38. Dark Violet
39. Baby Blue
40. Sky Blue
41. Light Blue
42. Medium Blue
43. Blue
44. Dark Blue
45. Navy Blue
46. Beige
47. Light Gray
48. Medium Gray
49. Gray
50. Dark Gray

1. Black
2. Golden
3. Light Red
4. Medium Red
5. Red
6. Dark Red
7. Lemon Yellow
8. Light Yellow
9. Yellow
10. Dark Yellow
11. Bright Orange
12. Light Orange
13. Medium Orange
14. Orange
15. Dark Orange
16. Chocolate
17. Light Brown
18. Medium Brown
19. Brown
20. Dark Brown
21. Neon Green
22. Light Green
23. Medium Green
24. Green
25. Army Green
26. Dark Green
27. Peach
28. Light Pink
29. Medium Pink
30. Pink
31. Hot Pink
32. Dark Pink
33. Medium Purple
34. Purple
35. Light Violet
36. Soft Violet
37. Violet
38. Dark Violet
39. Baby Blue
40. Sky Blue
41. Light Blue
42. Medium Blue
43. Blue
44. Dark Blue
45. Navy Blue
46. Beige
47. Light Gray
48. Medium Gray
49. Gray
50. Dark Gray

1. Black
2. Golden
3. Light Red
4. Medium Red
5. Red
6. Dark Red
7. Lemon Yellow
8. Light Yellow
9. Yellow
10. Dark Yellow
11. Bright Orange
12. Light Orange
13. Medium Orange
14. Orange
15. Dark Orange
16. Chocolate
17. Light Brown
18. Medium Brown
19. Brown
20. Dark Brown
21. Neon Green
22. Light Green
23. Medium Green
24. Green
25. Army Green
26. Dark Green
27. Peach
28. Light Pink
29. Medium Pink
30. Pink
31. Hot Pink
32. Dark Pink
33. Medium Purple
34. Purple
35. Light Violet
36. Soft Violet
37. Violet
38. Dark Violet
39. Baby Blue
40. Sky Blue
41. Light Blue
42. Medium Blue
43. Blue
44. Dark Blue
45. Navy Blue
46. Beige
47. Light Gray
48. Medium Gray
49. Gray
50. Dark Gray

1. Black
2. Golden
3. Light Red
4. Medium Red
5. Red
6. Dark Red
7. Lemon Yellow
8. Light Yellow
9. Yellow
10. Dark Yellow
11. Bright Orange
12. Light Orange
13. Medium Orange
14. Orange
15. Dark Orange
16. Chocolate
17. Light Brown
18. Medium Brown
19. Brown
20. Dark Brown
21. Neon Green
22. Light Green
23. Medium Green
24. Green
25. Army Green
26. Dark Green
27. Peach
28. Light Pink
29. Medium Pink
30. Pink
31. Hot Pink
32. Dark Pink
33. Medium Purple
34. Purple
35. Light Violet
36. Soft Violet
37. Violet
38. Dark Violet
39. Baby Blue
40. Sky Blue
41. Light Blue
42. Medium Blue
43. Blue
44. Dark Blue
45. Navy Blue
46. Beige
47. Light Gray
48. Medium Gray
49. Gray
50. Dark Gray

1. Black

2. Golden

3. Light Red

4. Medium Red

5. Red

6. Dark Red

7. Lemon Yellow

8. Light Yellow

9. Yellow

10. Dark Yellow

11. Bright Orange

12. Light Orange

13. Medium Orange

14. Orange

15. Dark Orange

16. Chocolate

17. Light Brown

18. Medium Brown

19. Brown

20. Dark Brown

21. Neon Green

22. Light Green

23. Medium Green

24. Green

25. Army Green

26. Dark Green

27. Peach

28. Light Pink

29. Medium Pink

30. Pink

31. Hot Pink

32. Dark Pink

33. Medium Purple

34. Purple

35. Light Violet

36. Soft Violet

37. Violet

38. Dark Violet

39. Baby Blue

40. Sky Blue

41. Light Blue

42. Medium Blue

43. Blue

44. Dark Blue

45. Navy Blue

46. Beige

47. Light Gray

48. Medium Gray

49. Gray

50. Dark Gray

1. Black
2. Golden
3. Light Red
4. Medium Red
5. Red
6. Dark Red
7. Lemon Yellow
8. Light Yellow
9. Yellow
10. Dark Yellow
11. Bright Orange
12. Light Orange
13. Medium Orange
14. Orange
15. Dark Orange
16. Chocolate
17. Light Brown
18. Medium Brown
19. Brown
20. Dark Brown
21. Neon Green
22. Light Green
23. Medium Green
24. Green
25. Army Green
26. Dark Green
27. Peach
28. Light Pink
29. Medium Pink
30. Pink
31. Hot Pink
32. Dark Pink
33. Medium Purple
34. Purple
35. Light Violet
36. Soft Violet
37. Violet
38. Dark Violet
39. Baby Blue
40. Sky Blue
41. Light Blue
42. Medium Blue
43. Blue
44. Dark Blue
45. Navy Blue
46. Beige
47. Light Gray
48. Medium Gray
49. Gray
50. Dark Gray

1. Black
2. Golden
3. Light Red
4. Medium Red
5. Red
6. Dark Red
7. Lemon Yellow
8. Light Yellow
9. Yellow
10. Dark Yellow
11. Bright Orange
12. Light Orange
13. Medium Orange
14. Orange
15. Dark Orange
16. Chocolate
17. Light Brown
18. Medium Brown
19. Brown
20. Dark Brown
21. Neon Green
22. Light Green
23. Medium Green
24. Green
25. Army Green
26. Dark Green
27. Peach
28. Light Pink
29. Medium Pink
30. Pink
31. Hot Pink
32. Dark Pink
33. Medium Purple
34. Purple
35. Light Violet
36. Soft Violet
37. Violet
38. Dark Violet
39. Baby Blue
40. Sky Blue
41. Light Blue
42. Medium Blue
43. Blue
44. Dark Blue
45. Navy Blue
46. Beige
47. Light Gray
48. Medium Gray
49. Gray
50. Dark Gray

1. Black
2. Golden
3. Light Red
4. Medium Red
5. Red
6. Dark Red
7. Lemon Yellow
8. Light Yellow
9. Yellow
10. Dark Yellow
11. Bright Orange
12. Light Orange
13. Medium Orange
14. Orange
15. Dark Orange
16. Chocolate
17. Light Brown
18. Medium Brown
19. Brown
20. Dark Brown
21. Neon Green
22. Light Green
23. Medium Green
24. Green
25. Army Green
26. Dark Green
27. Peach
28. Light Pink
29. Medium Pink
30. Pink
31. Hot Pink
32. Dark Pink
33. Medium Purple
34. Purple
35. Light Violet
36. Soft Violet
37. Violet
38. Dark Violet
39. Baby Blue
40. Sky Blue
41. Light Blue
42. Medium Blue
43. Blue
44. Dark Blue
45. Navy Blue
46. Beige
47. Light Gray
48. Medium Gray
49. Gray
50. Dark Gray

1. Black
2. Golden
3. Light Red
4. Medium Red
5. Red
6. Dark Red
7. Lemon Yellow
8. Light Yellow
9. Yellow
10. Dark Yellow
11. Bright Orange
12. Light Orange
13. Medium Orange
14. Orange
15. Dark Orange
16. Chocolate
17. Light Brown
18. Medium Brown
19. Brown
20. Dark Brown
21. Neon Green
22. Light Green
23. Medium Green
24. Green
25. Army Green
26. Dark Green
27. Peach
28. Light Pink
29. Medium Pink
30. Pink
31. Hot Pink
32. Dark Pink
33. Medium Purple
34. Purple
35. Light Violet
36. Soft Violet
37. Violet
38. Dark Violet
39. Baby Blue
40. Sky Blue
41. Light Blue
42. Medium Blue
43. Blue
44. Dark Blue
45. Navy Blue
46. Beige
47. Light Gray
48. Medium Gray
49. Gray
50. Dark Gray

1. Black
2. Golden
3. Light Red
4. Medium Red
5. Red
6. Dark Red
7. Lemon Yellow
8. Light Yellow
9. Yellow
10. Dark Yellow
11. Bright Orange
12. Light Orange
13. Medium Orange
14. Orange
15. Dark Orange
16. Chocolate
17. Light Brown
18. Medium Brown
19. Brown
20. Dark Brown
21. Neon Green
22. Light Green
23. Medium Green
24. Green
25. Army Green
26. Dark Green
27. Peach
28. Light Pink
29. Medium Pink
30. Pink
31. Hot Pink
32. Dark Pink
33. Medium Purple
34. Purple
35. Light Violet
36. Soft Violet
37. Violet
38. Dark Violet
39. Baby Blue
40. Sky Blue
41. Light Blue
42. Medium Blue
43. Blue
44. Dark Blue
45. Navy Blue
46. Beige
47. Light Gray
48. Medium Gray
49. Gray
50. Dark Gray

ENJOY BONUS
IMAGES FROM SOME
OF OUR
OTHER FUN
COLOR BY NUMBER
BOOKS!

FIND ALL OF OUR
BOOKS
ON AMAZON

Cactus and Succulent Coloring Book
Color By Numbers For Adults
Desert Plants Mosaic Puzzles

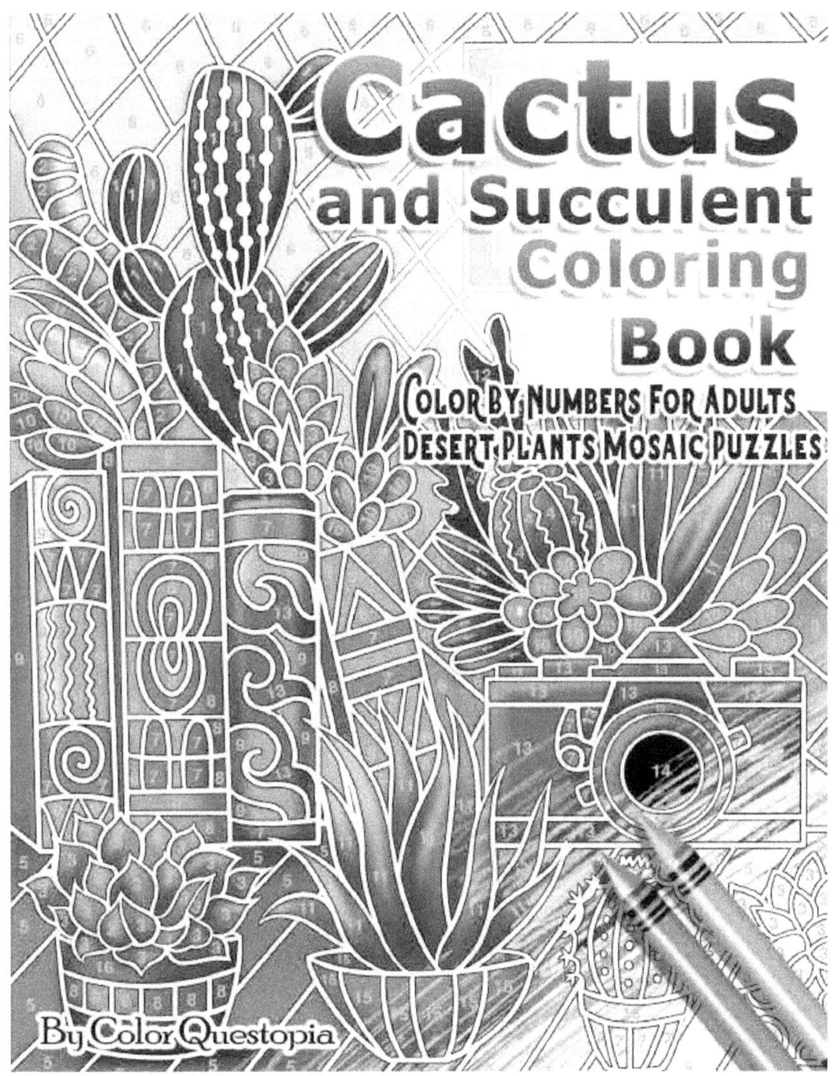

1. Light Orange

2. Pink

3. Green

4. Red

5. Light Yellow

6. Medium Green

7. Dark Green

8. Light Green

9. Dark Orange

10. Hot Pink

11. Yellow

12. Dark Pink

13. Light Violet

14. Dark Violet

15. Orange

16. Blue

17. Dark Blue

18. Light Brown

19. Sky Blue

Truck Coloring Book
Simple and Easy Mosaic
Color By Number

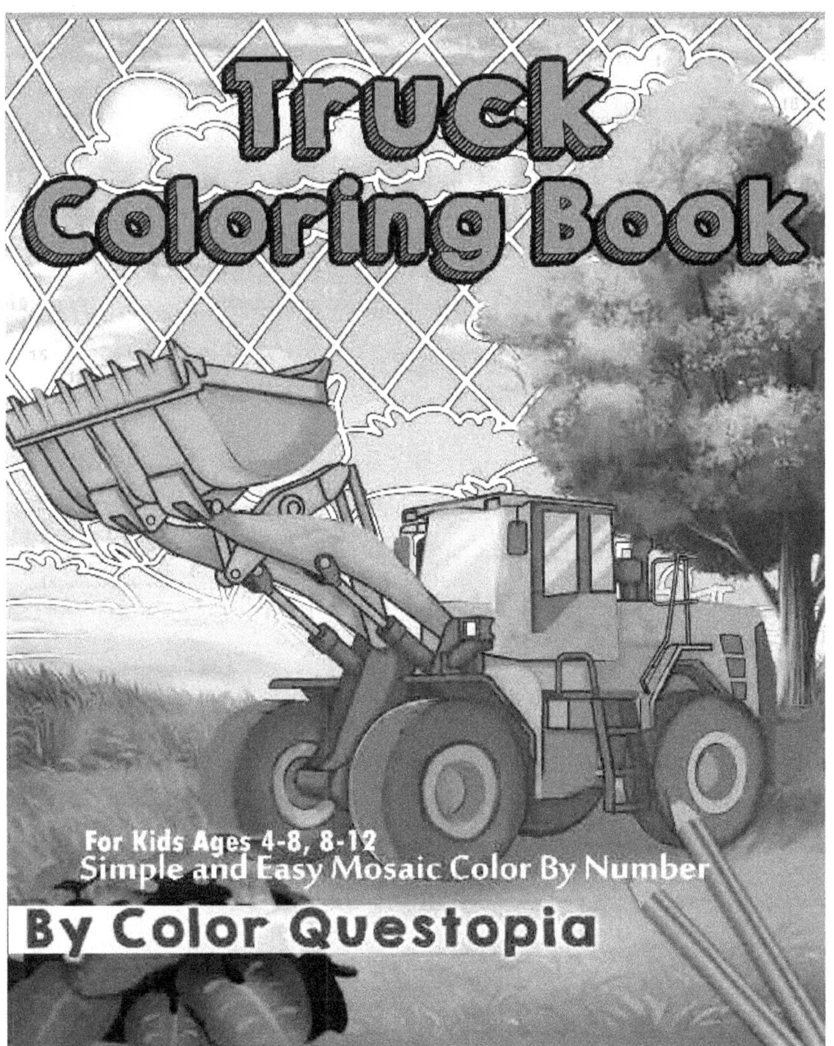

1. Blue

2. Yellow

3. Medium Blue

4. Purple

5. Dark Gray

6. Orange

7. Green

8. Dark Green

9. Light Brown

10. Light Green

11. Gray

12. Medium Gray

13. Light Gray

14. Baby Blue

15. White

16. Sky Blue

Beach Coloring Book
Large Print Summer Fun
Mosaic Color By Numbers

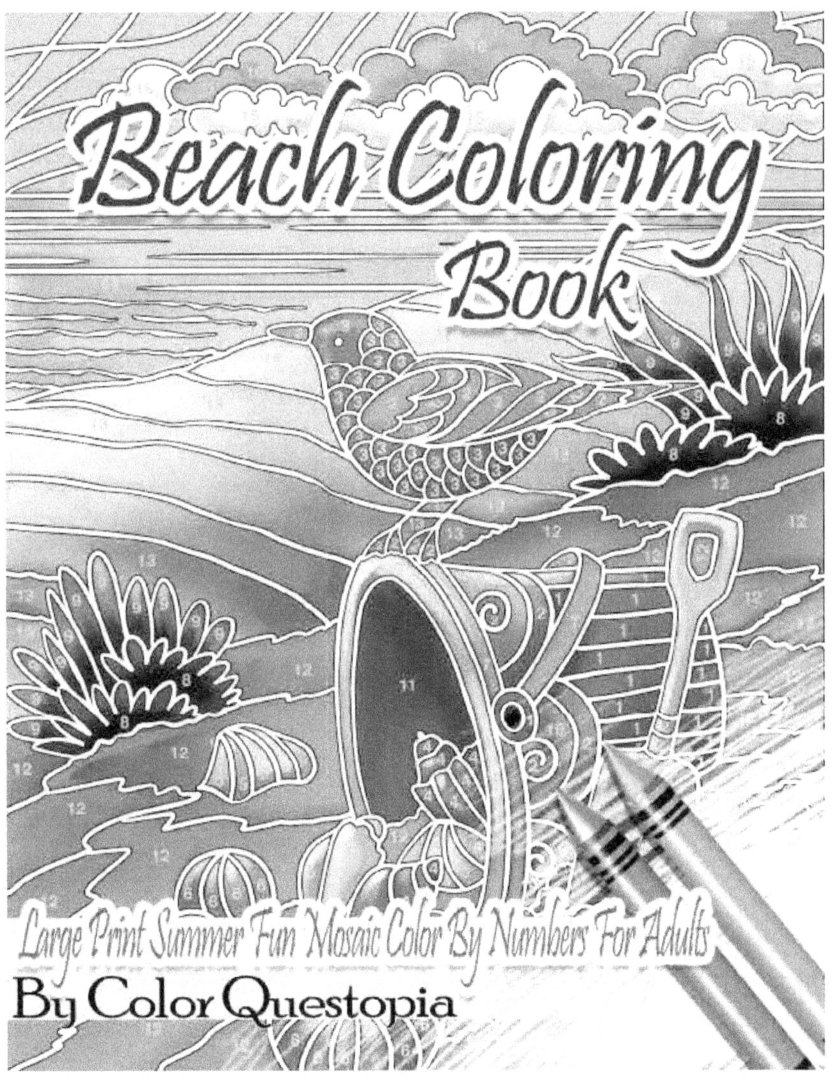

1. Pink

2. Yellow

3. Light Pink

4. Light Brown

5. Orange

6. Dark Yellow

7. Blue

8. Medium Green

9. Light Green

10. Dark Green

11. Green

12. Army Green

13. Peach

14. Light Gray

15. Light Yellow

16. Beige

17. Baby Blue

18. Sky Blue

Backyard Bugs Color by Numbers
Insect Coloring Book
For Kids and Toddlers

1. White

2. Black

3. Yellow

4. Baby Blue

5. Orange

6. Light Pink

7. Peach

8. Neon Green

9. Green

10. Army Green

11. Red

12. Light Violet

13. Sky Blue

Dragon Fantasy
Mosaic Color By Number
Black Background

1. Black

2. Bright Orange

3. Light Yellow

4. Light Brown

5. Beige

6. Yellow

7. Chocolate

8. Pink

9. Red

10. Brown

11. Medium Brown

12. Dark Brown

13. Medium Orange

14. Bright Orange

15. Light Orange

16. Dark Yellow

17. Soft Violet

18. Baby Blue

Please
Leave
Us
A Review
On Amazon

www.ingramcontent.com/pod-product-compliance
Lightning Source LLC
Chambersburg PA
CBHW081243250726
48654CB00012B/1465